Look, Find & Learn

Science & Nature

Illustrator: Tom Barrett

Writer: Katie John Sharp

Consultant: Michael Leyden, Ed.D.

Louis Weber, CEO
Publications International, Ltd.
7373 North Cicero Avenue
Lincolnwood, Illinois 60712

Permission is never granted for commercial purposes.

Manufactured in USA.

8 7 6 5 4 3 2 1

ISBN: 1-4127-1046-4

Publications International, Ltd.

Contents

Uncover the Secrets of the Universe

LOOK at amazing illustrations of natural wonders and scientific discoveries...**FIND** all kinds of things hidden in each picture...and **LEARN** tons of cool facts about science and nature—all in one awesome book! *Look, Find & Learn: Science & Nature* gives the lowdown on some of the coolest things in science, from creepy-crawly insects and mammoth dinosaurs to innovative inventions and space technology.

Each illustration is bursting with hidden items for you to discover. Some will be easy to spot, while others will require more effort—and maybe even a magnifying glass! Surrounding each colorful scene are smaller pictures with fascinating facts that make each search a fun learning experience. The facts will make the most

sense if you start in the top left corner and continue reading counterclockwise.

Keep in mind that no actual landscape would be this crowded with insects or animals. We've altered nature just a bit so we could pack in as much information as possible—and add even more fun for you! For example, in the dinosaur illustration, you'll find dinosaurs together that weren't actually alive at the same time.

Often you'll be asked to find more than one of the same thing. Even items that are only partly shown should be counted. If you're completely stumped, turn to pages 26–31 for the answers. When you've found everything and want more, turn to page 32 for more challenges!

So start looking, finding, and learning—the fun will never end!

OUT OF THIS WORLD!

Look up in the night sky. What do you spy? Do you see the moon and the stars? On some nights you might even see a few planets, a comet, and a meteor shower. But there is so much more in our solar system that you can't see with the naked eye. Stare into the space below to learn some of the secrets of the universe!

The Sun is the center of our solar system. All the planets and other objects in space *orbit*, or circle around, it. The Sun, which is a star, makes life on Earth possible because it gives off great amounts of light and heat. You'll be a star if you can find the star of our solar system.

Our home, planet Earth, is the third planet from the sun. You might think Earth is perfectly round, but it actually bulges slightly in the middle. This bulge is so small, however, that the planet appears round when you look at it in pictures. Who's having a ball with Earth?

Some people think Saturn runs rings around the other planets. Why? Because of its rings! While Jupiter, Neptune, and Uranus also have rings, Saturn's rings are much easier to see. Do you think they're easy to see in this scene?

Mercury is the planet closest to the Sun. This makes Mercury one hot spot! You can sometimes see Mercury in the western sky after sunset or in the eastern sky before sunrise. You'll be a hot shot if you can spot Mercury.

During the summer of 2003, the National Aeronautics and Space Administration (NASA) sent two robotic explorers, Spirit and Opportunity, to Mars. Thanks to these little robots, scientists have learned a lot about the Red Planet. Take this opportunity to find Spirit.

Jupiter is the largest planet in our solar system. It is wider than 11 Earths placed side by side! Jupiter's most striking feature is called the Giant Red Spot. It is formed from circulating gases that resemble a huge hurricane. Let's see if you can spot the Giant Red Spot.

Can you imagine a telescope the size of a school bus? Believe it or not, the Hubble Telescope is about that big. This special space-based telescope provides a clear view of objects that cannot be seen through telescopes on Earth. Is it clear to you where the Hubble is here?

Would you like to be a space traveler? Some astronauts explore space in the space shuttle. This space vehicle takes off like a rocket and lands like an airplane. You'll have a blast finding three space shuttles in this picture.

Earth isn't the only planet with a moon. Some planets even have more than one. Saturn, for example, has at least 30 moons! You'll be over the moon when you find six moons in this scene.

Neptune is called the Blue Planet. Storms with winds up to 400 miles per hour have lasted hundreds of years on Neptune. You'll be blue if you can't find the Blue Planet.

You'll have tons of fun searching for the items in each scene. Remember to start in the top left corner and read counterclockwise.

Animals may look different from one another, but they do have one thing in common: They all follow a sequence of changes called a *life cycle*. They begin life, change, and grow. Then they bring about a new generation, starting the cycle all over again. Are you ready to ride the cycle of life? Hold on to your helmet, and check out what's happening!

Staying alive is an important part of an animal's life cycle. Different animals have different ways to protect themselves. For example, a turtle can draw its head and legs into its shell for protection. Come out of your shell to find the turtle hiding here. It's a game of animal hide-and-seek!

Metamorphosis (meh-tuh-MOR-fuh-sus) is the word scientists use to describe the changes that animals experience from the time they hatch to adulthood. A tadpole is born with gills and no legs. Over time, it metamorphoses into a frog with legs and lungs. Hop to it: Find three tadpoles and three frogs.

Birds hatch from eggs. They are the only animals with feathers, which they use for flight and warmth. You'll be tickled if you can find the feather.

Parent birds keep their eggs warm until they hatch. The parents also bring food to the young until they're old enough to fly. Look high and low for the bird that just found dinner.

Lizards, snakes, and turtles are reptiles. Reptiles have dry, scaly skin and hatch from eggs. They are cold-blooded, which means their body temperature changes as the temperature around them changes. Shine a light on the lizard basking in the sun.

It's no yolk—reptiles lay their eggs on land. They may leave them in rotten wood or in a hole in the ground. Heat from the sun keeps the eggs warm until they hatch. Take a crack at finding five reptile eggs.

Fish may swim in schools, but mammals tend to train their young more than other animals do. Mammals protect and care for their babies until they can survive on their own. One way they do this is by nursing them. Can you sneak a peek at this mammal mommy and her hungry babies?

You can count on scientists to put animals that have similar features into groups. There are about 21,000 kinds of fish; 4,000 kinds of amphibians; 6,500 kinds of reptiles; 9,700 kinds of birds; and 4,500 kinds of mammals. Can we count on you to find the mammal that seems more like a bird?

Fish have gills so that they can live their entire lives in water. They hatch from eggs and are covered with tiny scales. Can you catch the fish out of water?

Amphibians live part of their lives in water and part on land. Their babies hatch from eggs and have gills for living in water. Over time, they develop lungs for breathing on land. Salamanders are amphibians. Can you find two in this scene?

Crawling with Bugs

Do insects bug you? Yes, some insects bite or sting, eat our food and clothes, and buzz in our ears. But insects actually do many good things for us. Some help make flowers and other plants. Others make honey and silk. And many insects are food for other animals. So before you swat that fly or stomp that ant, take a closer look inside the world of insects.

When you think of insects, you might think of spiders. But spiders aren't insects. They actually belong to a group called *arachnids*. Arachnids have eight legs, two body segments, and no antennae. Don't get "stuck" looking for the spider in its web.

Bees eat a sweet liquid called *nectar,* which is made by flowers. While they buzz from flower to flower to collect nectar, pollen sticks to their hind legs. This pollen then rubs off on other flowers, enabling them to produce seeds. Get "buzzy" and find a bee collecting nectar from this flower.

Ants are busy little insects. They work together to build their colonies; each ant has its own job. All of the ants' activities are for one purpose: to protect and feed the queen. The queen is responsible for laying eggs and finding new nests. Have you seen the queen in this scene?

You'll have to look very closely to find the Indian walkingstick. This slow-moving insect looks just like a twig. Its eggs are well hidden too; they look like brown seeds.

Butterflies have a four-stage life cycle. At the larval stage, they are known as caterpillars. Before the pupa stage, a caterpillar attaches to a twig or the underside of a leaf and makes a hard shell, or *cocoon,* around itself. Spread your wings and find the five caterpillars in this scene.

Did you know that only female mosquitoes drink blood? When she strikes, a mosquito injects a substance into the skin to keep the blood flowing—this is also what makes us itch! You'll have to move quickly to find the mosquito that's about to bite.

No bones about it—an insect's skeleton is on the outside of its body. That's why it's called an *exoskeleton.* As it grows, an insect sheds its skeleton to grow a new, larger one. Find the skeleton that's missing a bug.

While they do hop, grasshoppers fly and walk, too. These green or brown insects use their long back legs for hopping and their short front legs for holding prey and walking. Male grasshoppers also make noise by rubbing their back legs together. Hop to it and find seven grasshoppers.

Did you know that the ladybug is a beetle? You've probably seen a two-spotted ladybug before. It is orange-red with two black spots. This beetle is helpful to gardeners because it eats many garden pests. Can you spot 2 two-spotted ladybugs?

Time flies when you're having fun. Just ask a mayfly. As adults, mayflies live only a few days or hours. In fact, most adult insects live only a very short time. Put your eye on this mayfly.

Dragonflies are beautiful insects with long, slender bodies and four delicate wings. Their bodies may be red, green, or blue. Dragonflies eat other insects, sometimes catching them while flying. Find the dragonfly that's eating the fly.

Where Land Meets the Sea

Quick! Take a look at this tide pool off the Galapagos (guh-lah-puh-gohs) Islands. What's the hurry? In just hours, this unique habitat will look completely different. Tide pools occur where land meets the sea. At high tide, seawater covers the land, bringing living things with it. When the tide goes out, there's no telling what will be left behind.

Hermit crabs don't have shells of their own. Instead, they find empty snail shells and move right in. As hermit crabs grow, they move into bigger and bigger shells. Get moving and find the hermit crab without a shell.

Step on it: Catch two red-footed boobies. These diving birds get their name from the Spanish word *bobo*, which means stupid. Sailors gave the birds this name because they were easy to catch.

Tide pools are tied to the *tide,* a rising and falling of water in the ocean. At certain times of the day, the waters of the ocean get higher near the shore. At other times, they get lower. Tide pools form at high tide. Do you see three snails out of water? They were left high and dry by the tide.

The Galapagos Islands consist of 13 major islands in the Pacific Ocean west of Ecuador. They are actually the peaks of dormant volcanoes. The land is covered with hardened lava, and animals are often seen sunbathing on the hot rocks. Don't blow your top trying to find a lounging lava lizard.

The sea anemone is no enemy. These colorful animals look like bright, beautiful flowers. They fasten themselves to rocks or shells. At low tide, they close up so they don't dry out. Can you find this anemone in a hurry?

The living things of a tide pool depend on each other to survive. If pollution kills off a plant or animal, others may die too. Help keep the tide pool tidy by finding three pieces of trash in this picture.

Hungry for a seawater salad? A tide pool is home to plants called sea cucumbers. "Lettuce" see if you can find one without too much trouble!

Barnacles don't move around. Instead, they "cement" themselves to rocks—or sometimes to whales or boats—and stay put forever. Can you stick around long enough to find ten barnacles?

British scientist Charles Darwin visited the Galapagos Islands in 1835. He discovered many amazing animals and learned a lot about how species change over millions of years. Follow in Darwin's footsteps and discover four giant tortoises.

Mussels are a type of *mollusk*—creatures that have a soft body protected by a shell. Mussels spin strong threads that help them cling to rocks. Flex your muscles and find six mussels.

Marine iguanas are found only on the Galapagos Islands. These strange-looking reptiles are the only lizards that are *marine,* or ocean, feeders. Don't get all wet searching for the iguana that has stopped for a bite to eat!

Lights, Camera, Action!

What's the weather today? You can ask, but you can't do anything about the answer. You have to live with the weather, whether it's a swirling snowstorm or an intense heat wave. But what if life were like the movies? Imagine being able to create any kind of weather you wanted. Take a look, and see what you could do.

Ever think you'd like to hide in a fluffy white cloud? Don't be fooled—clouds can't hold your weight. They're actually made of millions of tiny, cold water droplets as well as crystals of ice. Can you find this cloud?

The water droplets inside a cloud can get very cold. When temperatures drop below freezing, the drops turn into tiny pieces of ice, and the pieces fall to the ground as snowflakes. Did you know that no two snowflakes look exactly alike? That means you'll only find one snowflake that looks like this.

Lightning can be frightening! The lightning we see flashes from a cloud to the ground. But it can also jump from cloud to cloud. Bolt through this scene to find the lightning.

A hurricane is a strong, swirling storm that begins over a warm ocean and causes heavy rains and strong winds. During a hurricane, air pressure is very low. Air pressure can be measured with a special tool called a *barometer*. The pressure is on to find the barometer in this scene.

The heat is on! Ultraviolet (UV) light from the sun can cause your skin to burn. You can protect yourself from harmful UV rays by wearing sunscreen. Can you find four bottles of it without breaking a sweat?

Do you ever wonder about thunder? When lightning flashes, it heats the air around it. This makes the air expand. The sudden expansion of air makes a rumble, which we call *thunder*. You can't really see thunder, but you'll find the word *thunder* in two places here.

It's raining, it's pouring! Here's how it works: The sun heats water on the ground, and the water rises to the sky and makes clouds. Drops of water in the clouds stick together and fall to the ground as rain. Check the rain gauge to see if it has rained cats and dogs recently.

Tornadoes are strong columns of spinning winds that can twist at more than 300 miles per hour! Being prepared can make a big difference during a violent storm. Blow through this scene quickly to find these emergency supplies.

Temperature is a measure of how cold or warm the air is. A thermometer measures the temperature. Can you keep your cool while searching for three thermometers?

Have you gotten wind of this? The sun heats the surface of the earth unevenly. Air that is hot *expands,* or gets bigger, and is pushed up by cooler air from below. This movement of air is the wind. Run like the wind to find three weather vanes.

What Goes Up Must Come Down

Look around you. Water is everywhere. It falls from the sky as rain and snow. Oceans, lakes, and rivers are filled with water. You swim in water, you drink water, and you bathe in water. Where does all the water come from? And where does it go? Dive into this picture, and then you'll know!

Water can exist as a liquid, as a gas, or as a solid. Solid water is ice. You'll be cool if you can find the ice in this picture.

Earth has a limited amount of water. That's why *conserving,* or protecting, water is very important. One way to conserve water is to keep it clean. Find three things that don't belong in the water.

All life on Earth depends on water. Neither animals nor plants could survive long without it. You could live a few weeks without food, but you'd only survive about a week without water. Do you think you can find the animal that stopped for a drink?

Clouds are made of water droplets. Different types of clouds have different names. *Cumulus* clouds look like cotton candy. Is there a cumulus cloud in this picture?

Water droplets inside a cloud get bigger and bigger. Soon, they become so heavy, they fall as rain. If the air is really cold, the droplets turn into water crystals we call *snow.* Find the thermometer that says you won't see snow today.

When it rains, you might see a rainbow. A rainbow is an arc of colors that appears when sunlight reflects off raindrops. It is not an actual object in the sky that you can touch but a pattern of light. Can you find three rainbows in this picture?

When something is able to float on water, it is because the liquid pushes upward on the object. This is called a *buoyant force.* Canoes, kayaks, and other boats are buoyant, as long as they don't have any holes. Find the boat that just won't float.

Pour a glass of cold water, and soon your glass may be all wet. That's because the water makes the glass cold. This causes water vapor in the air to *condense,* or become liquid water, on the outside of the glass. Find the pitcher that's wet inside and out.

Plants add water to the air, too. After they take in water through their roots, plants pass the water out through their leaves as water vapor. A tree might give off 70 gallons of water a day! Plant yourself in this picture and pick out five pink flowers.

You can tell the rain to go away, but there is always water in the air. The heat energy we receive from the sun causes water from puddles, lakes, rivers, and oceans to *evaporate,* or change into water vapor. Make a splash by finding six puddles in a flash.

BODIES IN MOTION

Your body is an amazing piece of machinery. Equipped with muscles, bones, and joints, your body can take you where you want to go and help you do what you want to do. Want to run around the block? Your legs will take you there. Want to shoot some hoops? Your legs and arms will help you slam-dunk with style. Get in the game to find out more about how the body works.

Most of the muscles in the body are called *skeletal muscles* because they hold the bones of the skeleton together. The main job of skeletal muscles is to move the body. Muscle in and find someone making a muscle.

Your body will be in hot water if you don't drink water! Fluids are important for everything the body does. You need at least six cups of water a day. When you're active, your body loses water through sweat, so you need to drink even more. Find eight people who know water is where it's at!

Have you ever heard the expression "An apple a day keeps the doctor away"? This means that nutritious foods, such as fruits and vegetables, make your body healthy and strong. Keep your eyes peeled for seven apples in this scene.

Ligaments are strong tissues that connect bones at places called *joints*. People who are unusually limber have very flexible ligaments. Will you have to bend over backward to spot someone with flexible ligaments here?

Your skull is a hard, bony covering with a watery layer underneath. Its job is to protect your delicate brain from injury. But you have a job to do, too: Always wear a helmet when riding a bicycle, skateboard, or scooter. Use your head to find six helmets.

Your heart is the "heart" of the circulatory system. With each beat, this muscle pumps blood throughout your body, carrying nutrients and oxygen to all your different body parts. Get pumping—find the heart without missing a beat.

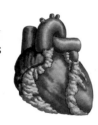

Tiny cells tell your brain about the world around you. Then your brain makes a split-second decision about how your body should respond. For example, if you touch something hot, your brain tells you to move your hand. Be a brain and find someone whose brain is saying, "Look out!"

At birth, the body has more than 300 bones and a lot of *cartilage,* a tough, rubbery tissue. As the body grows, most of the cartilage is replaced by bone. Also, many of the bones join together so adults have only 206 bones. Who probably has the most bones in this picture?

Bones are strong, but they can break. Someone with a broken bone, or *fracture,* is usually treated with a cast. A cast enables the bone to heal itself in the proper position. Bones can heal themselves because they are living tissue. Cast your eyes around the scene to find a bone on the mend.

Make no bones about it, bones give you shape. They support your body and protect organs such as your heart. Bones also store minerals, such as calcium, and release them into the body as needed. Find the bone that has no body.

OUT OF THIS WORLD!

Look up in the night sky. What do you spy? Do you see the moon and the stars? On some nights you might even see a few planets, a comet, and a meteor shower. But there is so much more in our solar system that you can't see with the naked eye. Stare into the space below to learn some of the secrets of the universe!

The Sun is the center of our solar system. All the planets and other objects in space *orbit,* or circle around, it. The Sun, which is a star, makes life on Earth possible because it gives off great amounts of light and heat. You'll be a star if you can find the star of our solar system.

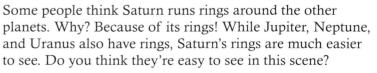

Our home, planet Earth, is the third planet from the sun. You might think Earth is perfectly round, but it actually bulges slightly in the middle. This bulge is so small, however, that the planet appears round when you look at it in pictures. Who's having a ball with Earth?

Some people think Saturn runs rings around the other planets. Why? Because of its rings! While Jupiter, Neptune, and Uranus also have rings, Saturn's rings are much easier to see. Do you think they're easy to see in this scene?

Would you like to be a space traveler? Some astronauts explore space in the space shuttle. This space vehicle takes off like a rocket and lands like an airplane. You'll have a blast finding three space shuttles in this picture.

Mercury is the planet closest to the Sun. This makes Mercury one hot spot! You can sometimes see Mercury in the western sky after sunset or in the eastern sky before sunrise. You'll be a hot shot if you can spot Mercury.

During the summer of 2003, the National Aeronautics and Space Administration (NASA) sent two robotic explorers, Spirit and Opportunity, to Mars. Thanks to these little robots, scientists have learned a lot about the Red Planet. Take this opportunity to find Spirit.

Jupiter is the largest planet in our solar system. It is wider than 11 Earths placed side by side! Jupiter's most striking feature is called the Giant Red Spot. It is formed from circulating gases that resemble a huge hurricane. Let's see if you can spot the Giant Red Spot.

Can you imagine a telescope the size of a school bus? Believe it or not, the Hubble Telescope is about that big. This special space-based telescope provides a clear view of objects that cannot be seen through telescopes on Earth. Is it clear to you where the Hubble is here?

Earth isn't the only planet with a moon. Some planets even have more than one. Saturn, for example, has at least 30 moons! You'll be over the moon when you find six moons in this scene.

Neptune is called the Blue Planet. Storms with winds up to 400 miles per hour have lasted hundreds of years on Neptune. You'll be blue if you can't find the Blue Planet.

A WALK ON THE WILD SIDE

You've gone back in time—back to the age of the dinosaurs! It's been millions of years since these fascinating creatures walked the planet. Back then, you wouldn't have found this many dinosaurs in one place or even all of these dinosaurs in the same time period. But we've brought them together to give you a chance to walk with the dinosaurs—without worrying about becoming dinner!

C If you were the first to discover a dinosaur, you would get to name it! When creating a name, scientists often use words that describe the animal's body or behavior. For example, *Brachyceratops* (BRAK-ee-SAIR-ah-tops) is a plant-eater whose name means "short-horned face." Horn your way into this scene to find the *Brachyceratops*.

T When you think of dinosaurs, you probably picture huge animals with sharp teeth. But not all dinosaurs were big. The meat-eater *Eoraptor* (ee-oh-RAP-tor) was only about the size of a dog! Will you have to work like a dog to find four *Eoraptors* in this scene?

T *Saltopus* (SAL-toh-pus) was not a salty octopus. Instead, this dinosaur, whose name means "hopping foot," was a tiny, fast-moving meat-eater. About the size of a cat, *Saltopus* was one of the smallest of all the dinosaurs. Hop to it and catch two of these tiny dinos.

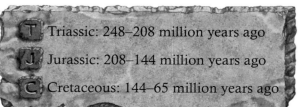

T Triassic: 248–208 million years ago

J Jurassic: 208–144 million years ago

C Cretaceous: 144–65 million years ago

J At 125 feet long, the *Seismosaurus* (SIZE-moh-SAWR-us) may have been one of the longest land animals ever! That's why its name means "earthquake lizard." How long will it take you to find this mover and shaker?

Is that a boat? A fish? Neither—it's a *Spinosaurus* (SPIE-noh-SAWR-us), a large dinosaur with spines nearly six feet long coming out of its back. Its saillike fin probably helped keep this meat-eater warm. Take a stab at spotting two of these spiny lizards.

Tyrannosaurus (tie-RAN-oh-SAWR-us) *rex*, or *T. rex*, means "tyrant lizard king." This dinosaur was one of the scariest meat-eaters of its time. It was about the length of a school bus and had sharp teeth and claws. Sink your teeth into this scene to find the *T. rex* that's using its teeth.

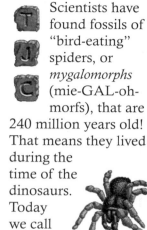

Scientists have found fossils of "bird-eating" spiders, or *mygalomorphs* (mie-GAL-oh-morfs), that are 240 million years old! That means they lived during the time of the dinosaurs. Today we call these spiders *tarantulas*. Spin your web around eight of these creepy crawlers.

Keep your eyes on the sky—there are flying reptiles, or pterosaurs (TAIR-oh-sawrs), up there! Pterosaurs were not dinosaurs, but they may have been distantly related to them. *Dsungaripterus* (jung-gah-RIP-ter-us) was one of the strangest-looking pterosaurs. You'll have to search the scene high and low if you want to find all eight.

Dinosaurs are closely related to birds. Many dinosaurs looked a lot like the birds you see today. For example, *Ornithomimus* (or-NITH-oh-MEEM-us) looked much like today's ostrich. Look for the *Ornithomimus* to see the resemblance.

Watch your legs around the *Ankylosaurus* (an-KEE-loh-SAWR-us). This well-known dinosaur swung its tail from side to side like a club. An *Ankylosaurus* was so strong, it could break the legs of an attacking dinosaur—ouch! Take a swing at finding the *Ankylosaurus* now.

Flower Power

It's apple season on the Fantastic Farm! Families come from near and far to pick juicy apples fresh from the trees. But that's not all that happens on this busy farm. The plant life here—and everywhere—produces lots of good things to eat and enjoy. Dig in to find out more!

You know animals have body parts, but did you know that plants have parts too? Important plant parts include the roots, the stem, the leaves, and the flowers. Each part plays a role in keeping the plant alive. Plant yourself in this scene to find the plant that's showing all its parts.

Most plants are flowering plants. These include the plants around your house, the vegetables and fruits you eat, wildflowers, and trees and bushes. Can you pick ten red flowers that look like this?

Evergreen trees stay green year-round. This is because they are constantly losing their sharp, thin needles and growing new ones. Poke around to find five evergreens.

Most seeds need soil, water, and light to help them grow. There are seven watering cans sprinkled around the farm. Can you find them?

20

BEECH

WILLOW

OAK

Deciduous trees shed their leaves every year, usually in the fall. Dropping their leaves is one way these trees prepare for winter. Willow, oak, and beech trees are all examples of deciduous trees. Drop what you're doing to find three oak leaves, three willow leaves, and three beech leaves.

Not all cones hold ice cream. *Conifers* are plants that make cones instead of flowers. Their seeds grow on the scales that make up their cones. Try to scoop up the eight cones that have fallen from their trees.

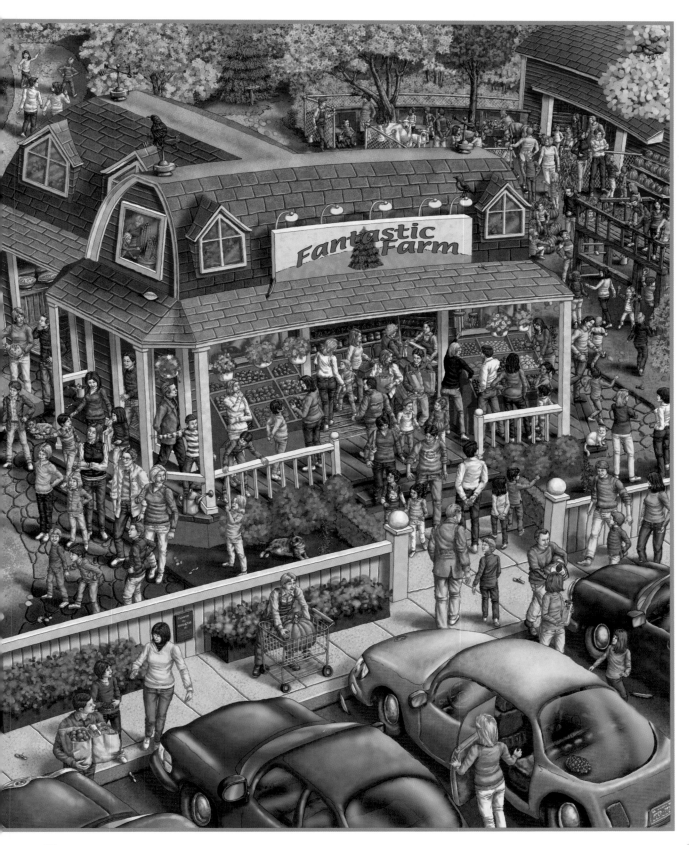

Some seeds have to "wing" their way to the ground. Maple, ash, and elm trees all have helicopterlike seeds that help them find a place to grow. Spin around and find eight maple seeds.

Birds help move seeds, too. They eat fruit, but their bodies don't digest the seeds. Instead, the seeds become part of their body waste. Birds may drop the seeds miles from the parent plant. Can you catch 12 birds in this picture?

Plants can't run and hide, and they can't call for help. However, they have other ways to protect themselves. A cactus, for example, has sharp points that keep animals away. Point out the cactus.

Have you ever wondered how seeds find a place to grow? The wind carries some seeds, such as those of dandelion plants and cottonwood trees. Blow through this scene to find someone helping the wind spread seeds.

INVENTION CONVENTION

Welcome to the Invention Convention! The students at this special science fair are showcasing the work of some of the greatest minds in history. Here you will find inventions that have made life easier, safer, and more enjoyable. Put your mind to work, and see what you can discover.

An inventor protects his or her creations by getting a patent. A patent is issued by the government, and it means only the inventor can sell that particular invention for a certain number of years. Can you point out the patent in this picture?

Tune in to Italian Guglielmo Marconi's (1874–1937) ground-breaking innovation. He was the first person to use wireless technology to send messages over long distances. His invention paved the way for radio and then television. Scan the scene to find three radios.

We'd be in the dark without Thomas Edison's (1847–1931) invention of the lightbulb. But did you know he also held more than 1,000 other patents? He had many ideas related to electricity, including lamp sockets, electricity meters, and safety fuses. Brighten your day by finding seven lightbulbs now!

When you turn on Thomas Edison's invention, it's another inventor's work that makes it glow. Nikola Tesla (1856–1943) developed systems that make and use an electric current known as alternating current (AC). Power through this scene to find the electric cord.

Inventions can sometimes be happy accidents. That was certainly the case for 11-year-old Frank Epperson (1894–?). He left a fruit drink out overnight with a stirrer in it. It froze, and the Epsicle was born. The name was later changed to *Popsicle.* Can you keep your cool while looking for the Popsicle in this scene?

Did you know there's a fiber that's five times stronger than steel? It's called Kevlar, and it was invented by Stephanie Louise Kwolek (1923—). Kevlar is used to make bulletproof vests, trampolines, helmets, and tennis rackets. Will you have a tough time finding the Kevlar in this scene?

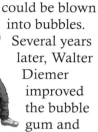

Chew on this: In 1906, inventor Frank Fleer developed the first chewing gum that could be blown into bubbles. Several years later, Walter Diemer improved the bubble gum and began selling it under the name *Dubble Bubble.* Find the bubble on the double!

You couldn't watch your favorite television shows if it weren't for Philo Taylor Farnsworth (1906–1971). He invented the technology that made television possible. What's more, he began his invention as a teenager! Stay tuned to find five televisions in this picture.

Does the name Alexander Graham Bell (1847–1922) ring a bell? This Scottish-born inventor and educator was the first person to successfully send human speech over wire. There are four telephones in this scene. Can you call them out?

To you, a peanut is just a peanut. But to George Washington Carver (1864–1943), the tasty little nut was so much more! This African-American scientist made more than 300 products from peanuts, including a milk substitute, printer's ink, and soap. Go nuts! Find the peanuts.

23

FANTASY ISLAND

Welcome to Fantasy Island! The plants and animals you'll find here are from different places all over the world but they have one thing in common—they're in danger of extinction. Scientists are working hard to help save these plants and animals. They hope to increase their numbers and teach people how they can help too.

The California condor once lived wild in southern California. Now this vulture is nearly extinct. Only about 150 exist, most in captivity. However, in 2004, three eggs hatched in the wild for the first time in years! "Eggs"amine the scene to find six condor eggs.

The black-footed ferret once scurried across North American prairies eating prairie dogs. But today this relative of the weasel is endangered. As prairie dogs became scarce (due to disease and attempts at population control), the number of black-footed ferrets dropped. Can you ferret out three black-footed ferrets?

You'll have to stay grounded if you want to find the kiwi here. That's because this chicken-size bird from New Zealand is flightless. Scientists call the kiwi an "honorary mammal" because of its hairy, ratlike appearance; catlike whiskers; and tendency to dig burrows. The kiwi now faces extinction due to predators and loss of habitat.

What happens if you only eat one thing and suddenly it's gone? You become endangered. That's what's happening to the bamboo-eating giant panda bear. These black-and-white Chinese bears are on the verge of extinction because their bamboo-forest homes are being destroyed. We'll "bear" with you while you search for two pandas.

Queen Alexandra's Birdwing Butterfly is the world's biggest butterfly. It has a wingspan of 10 inches or more! Unfortunately, this poisonous butterfly is in danger of extinction because its rain forest habitat is being destroyed. Float through this scene to find one male and one female Queen Alexandra's Birdwing Butterfly.

female

male

The bald eagle is the national bird of the United States. This bird of prey is a threatened species because people are tearing down its forest home to build farms and cities. Use your eagle eye to find three eagles.

The Knowlton cactus, which grows in Colorado and New Mexico, is endangered because people uproot it to sell or use in their personal cactus collections. Will you get stuck looking for the cactus?

The Siberian tiger is the largest of all the wildcats. Unfortunately, there are only about 400 left because people kill them for sport. These orange-brown and black meat-eaters kill their prey with a bite to the neck. Earn your stripes by catching two tigers.

Snakeroot is not an endangered animal; it's an endangered plant! This flowering plant got its name from its snakelike roots. People once used it to treat snakebites. Root around to find the snakeroot.

Snow leopards have beautiful spotted fur, which enables them to hide in the snow and among rocks to surprise their prey. Unfortunately, humans like snow leopards' fur so much, they've overhunted this wildcat. Can you spot a snow leopard?

The odd-looking two-toed sloth is the slowest animal on Earth. It spends most of its time hanging upside down in trees. The sloth is endangered because humans are destroying the forest it calls home. Will you have to turn this scene upside down to find the sloth?

	turtle		feather		fish out of water		birdlike mammal (bat)		reptile eggs
	tadpoles and frogs		bird with worm		salamander		nursing mammal		lizard

	spider in its web		Indian walkingstick		eating dragonfly		grasshopper		mosquito about to bite
	bee collecting nectar		mayfly		two-spotted ladybug		exoskeleton		caterpillar
	queen ant								

Tide Pools

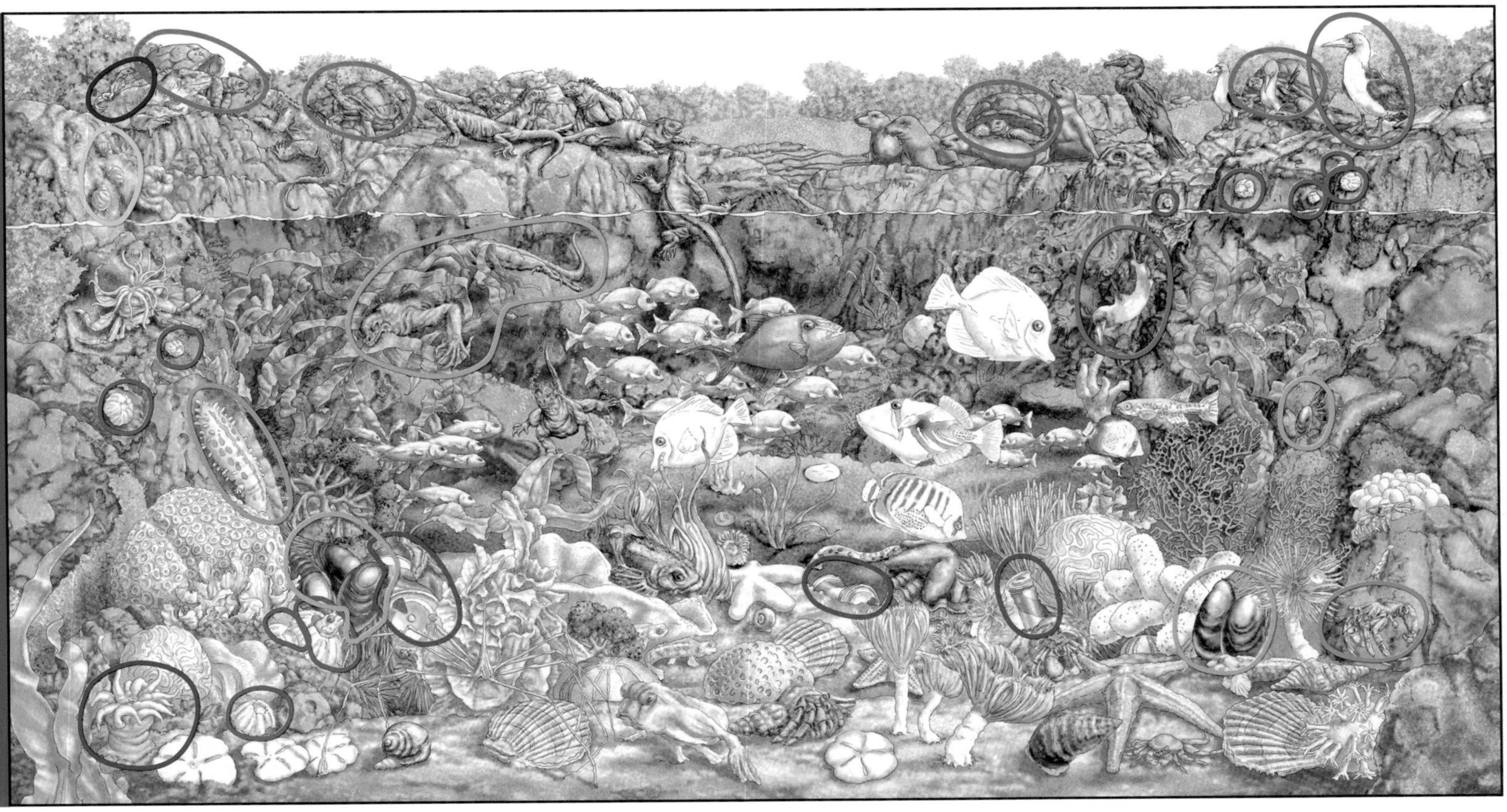

- hermit crab
- lava lizard
- marine iguana
- barnacles
- trash
- red-footed booby
- mussels
- tortoise
- sea cucumber
- sea anemone
- snails

Weather

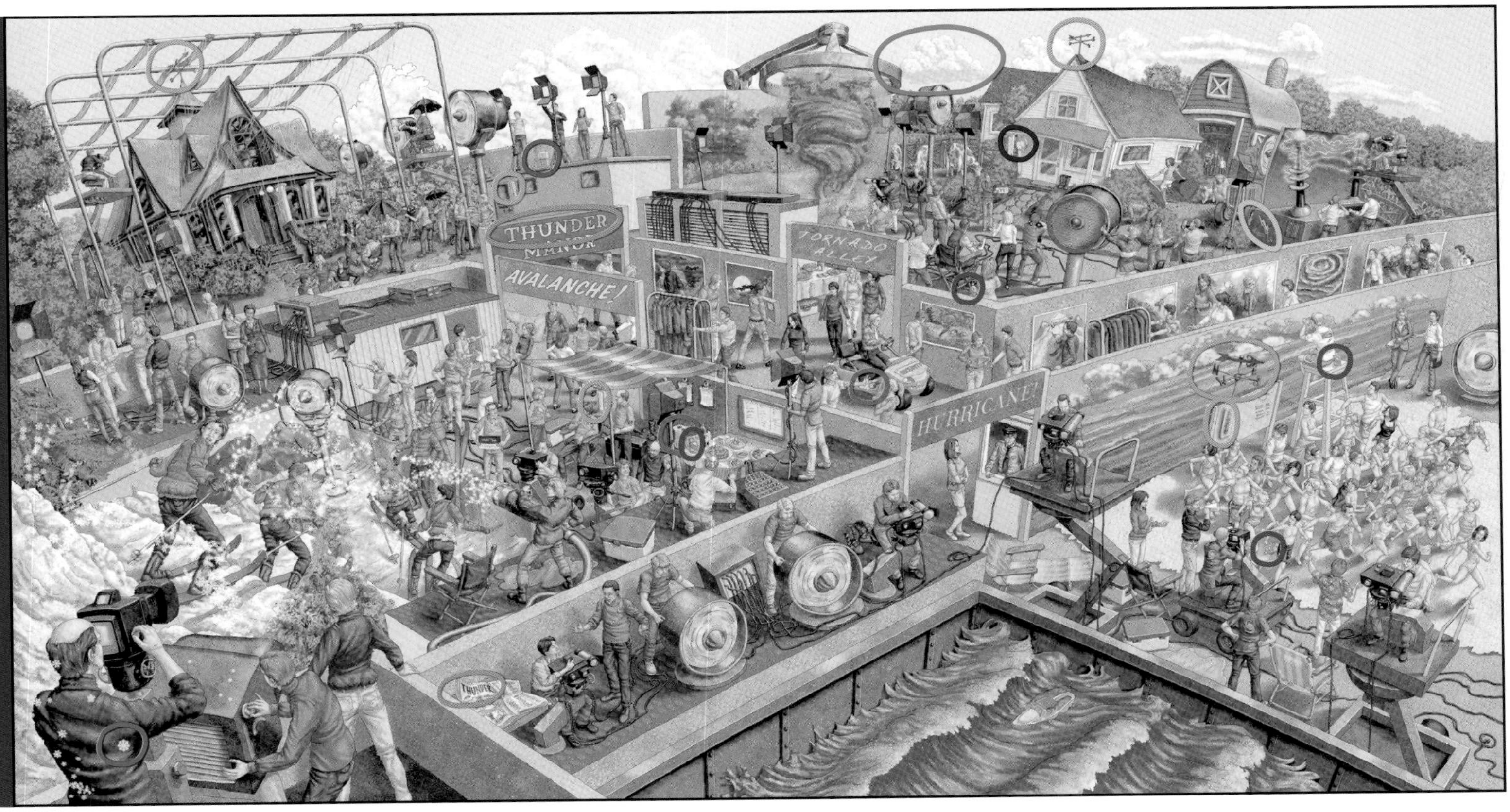

- cloud
- lightning
- thermometer
- emergency supplies
- thunder
- snowflake
- barometer
- weather vane
- rain gauge
- sunscreen

ice	squirrel	thermometer	pink flower	sinking boat
trash	cumulus cloud	puddle	pitcher	rainbow

person making muscle	apple	cast	baby	heart
water bottle	person with flexible ligaments	bone	brain	helmet

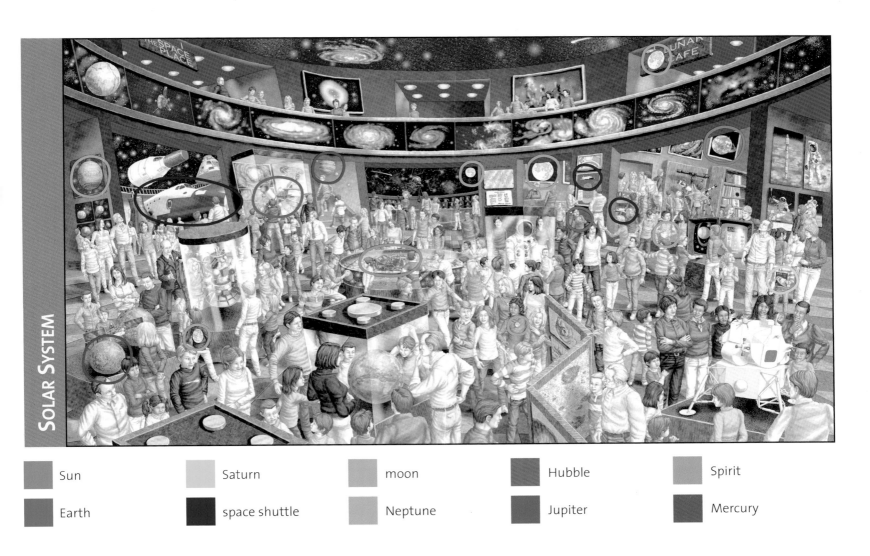

SOLAR SYSTEM

Sun	Saturn	moon	Hubble	Spirit
Earth	space shuttle	Neptune	Jupiter	Mercury

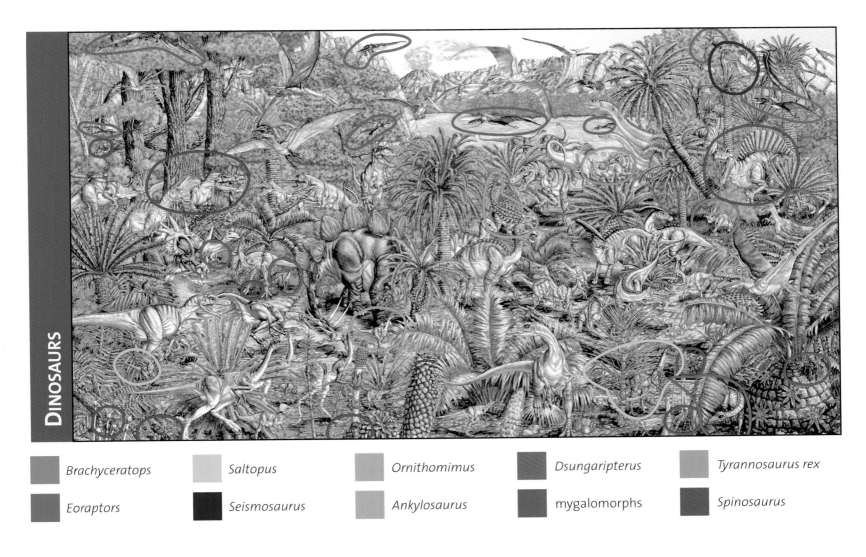

DINOSAURS

Brachyceratops	*Saltopus*	*Ornithomimus*	*Dsungaripterus*	*Tyrannosaurus rex*
Eoraptors	*Seismosaurus*	*Ankylosaurus*	*mygalomorphs*	*Spinosaurus*

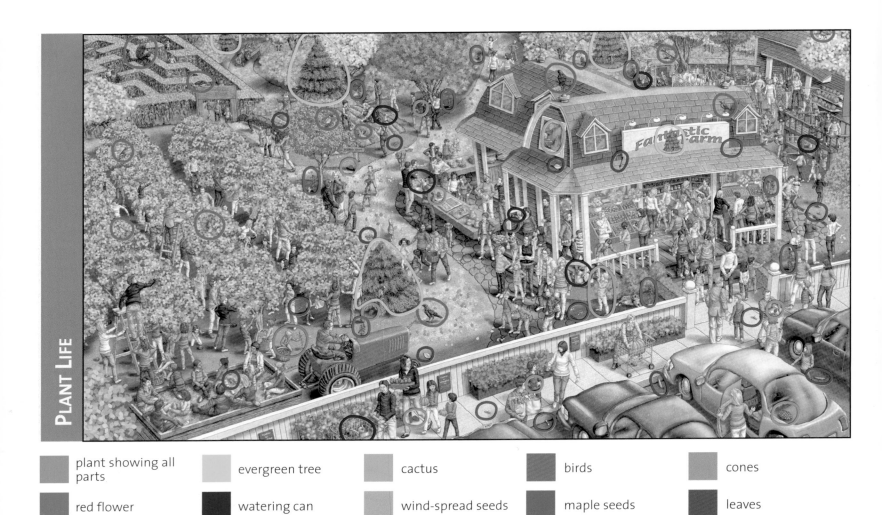

	plant showing all parts		evergreen tree		cactus		birds		cones
	red flower		watering can		wind-spread seeds		maple seeds		leaves

	patent		lightbulb		telephone		television		Kevlar (tennis racket)
	radio		electric cord		peanuts		child blowing bubble		Popsicle

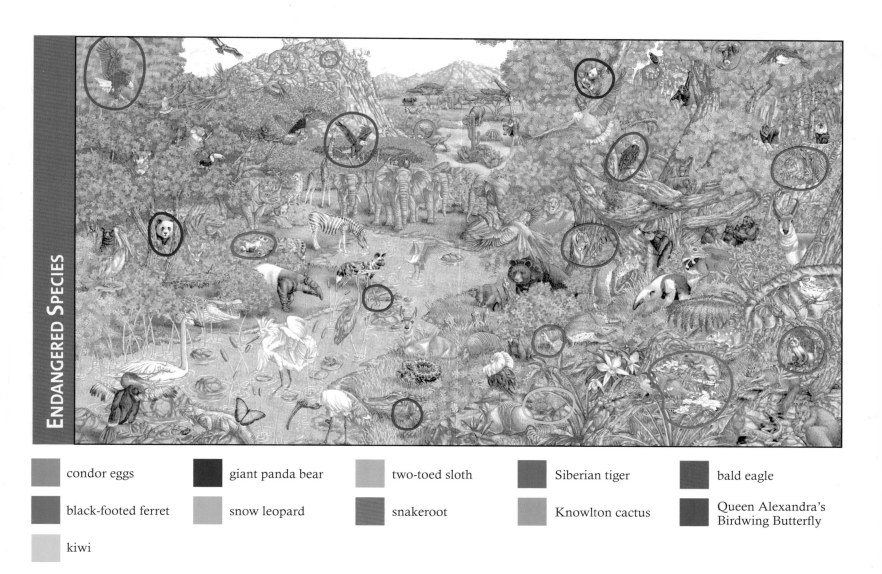

▨	condor eggs	▨	giant panda bear	▨	two-toed sloth	▨	Siberian tiger	▨	bald eagle
▨	black-footed ferret	▨	snow leopard	▨	snakeroot	▨	Knowlton cactus	▨	Queen Alexandra's Birdwing Butterfly
▨	kiwi								

Look, Find & Learn Even More!

Think that's all there is? Not so fast! There's plenty more for you to find within these pages. Take the plunge—explore the scenes again to discover these cool items!

ANIMALS

Many kinds of birds do not build nests for their eggs—they lay their eggs on the ground. Other birds nest in hollow trees, holes in the ground, or nests that other birds have left behind. Don't go away empty-handed—find the empty nest.

WATER CYCLE

Water exists in many forms on Earth, such as polar ice caps, glaciers, oceans, lakes, and underground water supplies. In fact, water covers 70 percent of Earth's surface. How many times can you find the word *water?*

WATER

DINOSAURS

The largest known dinosaur, called *Argentinosaurus* (AR-jen-teen-oh-SAWR-us), may have been as long as 100 feet or more. This plant-eater weighed a lot, too—about as much as 20 five-ton elephants! Step on it: find an Argentinosaurus footprint.

INSECTS

Insects are *arthropods*, a type of *invertebrate*. Invertebrates do not have backbones. Earthworms, snails, and many sea creatures are invertebrates. How quickly can you find three snails?

HUMAN BODY

If you lived to be 80 years old, your heart might beat around 3 billion times! You can figure out how many times your heart beats in one minute by taking your pulse. It beats faster or slower depending on your movement. Get moving—put your finger on someone taking his pulse.

PLANT LIFE

Most plants have roots that grow underground. Roots take in water and minerals that the plant needs to grow. But that's not all they do. They also keep the plant "rooted" in place. Root around and find a plant that's been uprooted.

TIDE POOLS

Sand dollars are coin-shape animals that live on the ocean floor. They are related to sea stars and sea urchins. If you break open a sand dollar, you'll find loose pieces inside. These are its teeth! Cash in on this clue: Five sand dollars are hiding here.

SOLAR SYSTEM

Comets are chunks of ice, dust, rock, and frozen gas. Comets form outside the solar system but are pulled in by the sun's gravity. Blast back to make heads or tails of the comet.

TECHNOLOGY

American Mary Anderson invented windshield wipers in 1903. Her invention was first used on streetcars. Ten years later, all cars had them. If you're not too wiped out, find Mary's wipers.

WEATHER

If you don't want to get your feet wet, you'd better look for four pairs of rain boots!

ENDANGERED SPECIES

There are many kinds of sea turtles, and all are endangered or threatened. People hunt these reptiles to make leather from their skin; they also steal their eggs. Do you see the sea turtle?

32